ANNIE THE AVALANCHE

A Rumbling and Rolling Adventure

Rana Boulos

Acknowledgements

"The simplification process in a children's picture book is what makes it the most interesting and delicate genre to write."

Rana Boulos

1. I would like to thank my family for supporting me through the self-publishing journey.

2. I would like to thank my editor Matt and my designer Raafia for their help and patience in getting this book completed.

ANNIE THE AVALANCHE

A Rumbling and Rolling Adventure

Book 5 of the Nature Speaks Series

eBook :	978-1-80352-131-2

Papaerback:	978-1-80352-132-9

Hard Cover:	978-1-80352-133-6

Publisher: Independent Publishing Network

Author: Rana Boulos

Illustrations & Formatting: Raafia Noor Afzal

First printing edition 2022.

Printed in the United States of America.

www.rana-boulos-author.com

Dedications

To my daughters Tamara and Chloe: you are
the source to my happiness and inspiration.
I am proud and blessed to be your mother.

To all the children of the world:
keep on blooming!

To all educators: words are not enough to
thank you for what you do.
You are simply amazing!

Trigger
Fresh snow layer
Crack!!!
Avalanche
Snow Slab
Weak Layer
Snow
Rock

Introduction:

This is a story about how Annie the Avalanche came to life. For an avalanche to be triggered, four factors are required: a steep slope, a snowpack, a weak layer in the snowpack, and a trigger.

The story begins with best friends Steve and Mark deciding to build the biggest snowball ever. The mountain slopes were already covered with several layers of snow; the top layer was fresh and dense, while the bottom layer was weak because the snowflakes did not stick together properly. This is explained by the fact that the snowflakes fight amongst themselves and do not want to join together. It is only when the snowball rolls down the slope that the avalanche is triggered. As soon as it reaches the weakened layer, a snow slab tears out of the top layer, collapses, and starts sliding down the snowy mountain at high speed, triggering the avalanche. The avalanche picks up speed, destroying entire trees that are buried by it, and engulfing the snowball and five mountain goats, who fortunately survive through survival tactics once the avalanche comes to a stop.

Trees

Goats

It was winter break and all sorts of families were spending the Christmas holiday at their favorite ski resort.

They had stayed indoors for two days straight because of a blizzard that brought with it a great amount of fresh snow.

The next morning, best friends Steve and Mark awoke very early. They looked out the window and saw that it had finally stopped snowing. They decided to head to the top one of the slopes near their chalet to build the biggest snowball ever. They slipped on their gloves and off they went.

"You scoop up the snow and I will pack it onto the snowball," Steve instructed. So the boys started building their snowball, scooping and packing, scooping and packing.

"Look at it grow!" exclaimed Mark. "It's going to be one BIG snowball."

There was an issue though. Far down the slope, a hidden trouble was growing beneath the fresh layer of snow.

Some snowflakes had gotten into a squabble and decided not to stick together as they normally would.

"Please don't fight," said one of the wiser snowflakes.

"Remember what Mama always told us?" She repeated her favorite quote that she would use whenever there was a squabble. "Friendship is the only cement that will ever hold the world together."

The snowflakes, however, did not want to listen to their wise friend.

"Get away from me!" cried one snowflake to another.

"Don't touch me!", screamed the other.

While their fight grew, Steve and Mark's snowball was now HUMONGOUS high above.

They were preparing to roll it down the slope.

The boys looked at one another, both grinning from ear to ear.

"Are you ready?" Mark asked Steve.

"I sure am!" replied Steve.

Together the boys shouted:

"Ready...

Get set...

GO!"

Down went the snowball rolling onto the slope, picking up speed.

"Look at it go!" shouted Steve.

"I hear some kind of rumbling," the snowflakes exclaimed. They were under the layer of fresh snow, but they could feel something coming.

"Quick, we need to bond together!" said the wise snowflake. "With our weakened state, there will be a disaster," she added.

CRRRAAACK!

But as soon as she said these words, the snowball came rolling on top of where the snowflakes were fighting. The snowflakes in the bottom layer were not able to bond in time and a slab from the top layer of snow cracked, collapsed, and started to slide downhill.

With the snow sliding at a terrible speed down the slope,
Annie the Avalanche came to life. Like a swelling cloud of
snow, growing each second, she rumbled down the slope,
burying everything in her path.

Further down, five mountain goats were hiking
from one mountain to another, looking for food.

Steve and Mark watched from afar as Annie the Avalanche gobbled up their snowball, entire trees, and the five mountain goats!

"Oh no!" cried Mark. "The goats are caught
in the avalanche!"

When Annie the Avalanche came to a halt, the mountain goats started thrashing about and paddling with their feet inside the snow. They "swam" towards the light and one by one, they made it to the surface.

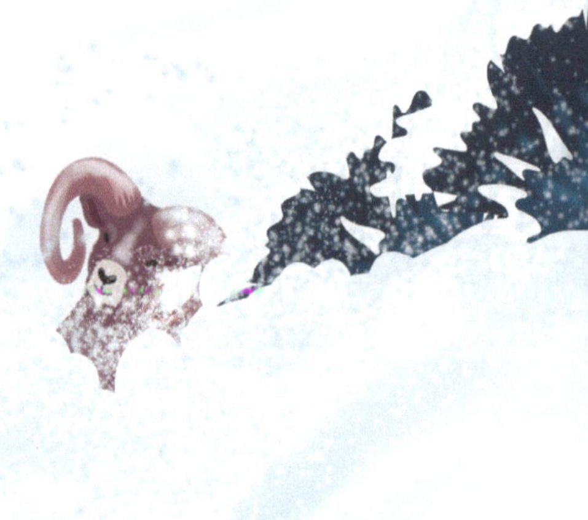

"Hooray!" shouted the boys. "The goats made it!"

"Our snowball, though, is history," said Steve.

And they both laughed.

The End

About the Author

So, who wrote this book? I'm Rana and this is my little dog Muscles in the photo. I have worked with children who are just like you for 30 years. I am also a mom and have two beautiful girls of my own. I come from a wonderful country called Canada and for 8 years, I've worked in a nursery that is  full of many different cultures in a land called the UAE. I love going to the beach, building sandcastles, and collecting seashells. I also love animals and I think my favourites might be either dogs or birds. I can also speak 7 languages - which I love - because it means that I can talk to people all over the world!

I've learned that picture books, just like mine, are a great way to help you understand the world that we live in. You are the inspiration for my books, and I only hope that they bring you endless joy!

Through the power of story and my degrees in Education and Modern Languages, I aim to bridge cultural divides and foster an understanding and a path to harmonious living for all children.

The inspiration for my stories comes from the children I teach and the amazing world around us.

Did you enjoy the story?

Please leave a review on Amazon.

It would mean the world to me!

For more information:

www.rana-boulos-author.com

https://www.facebook.com/ranaboulosauthor/

www.instagram.com/ranaboulosauthorltd/

You can get in touch at:

hello@rana-boulos-author.com